June 23, 2022 Thursday

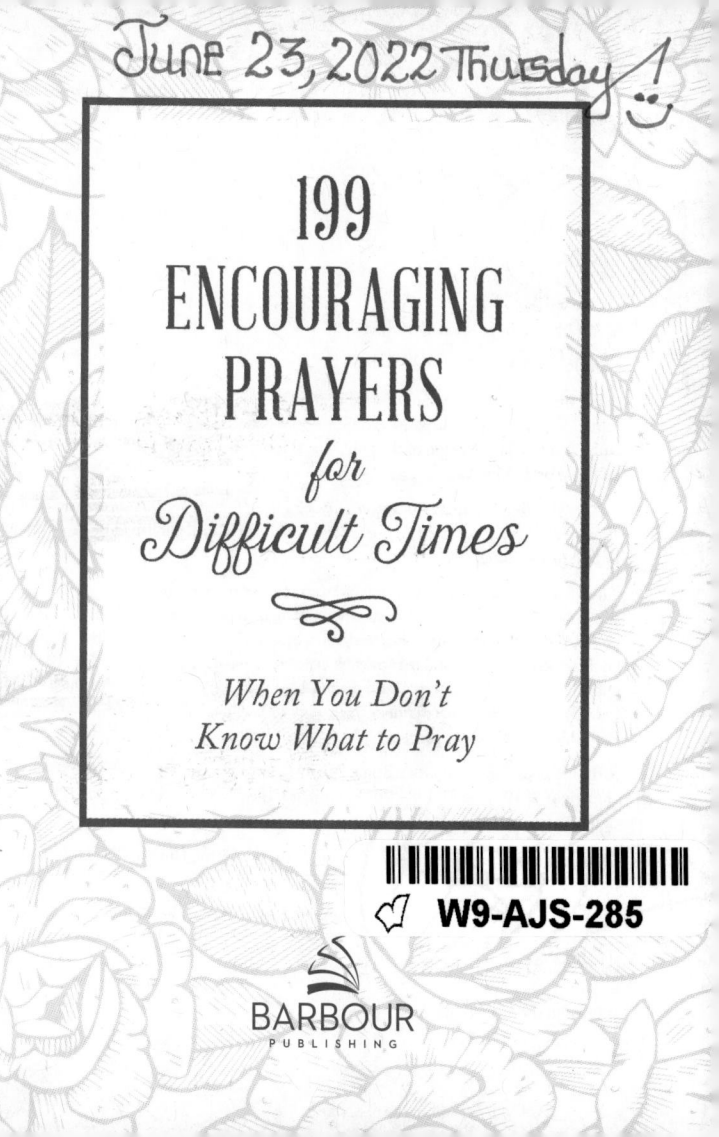

199
ENCOURAGING
PRAYERS
for
Difficult Times

*When You Don't
Know What to Pray*

W9-AJS-285

BARBOUR
PUBLISHING

Published by Barbour Publishing, Inc., 1810 Barbour Drive, Uhrichsville, Ohio
44683, www.barbourbooks.com

Our mission is to inspire the world with the life-changing message of the Bible.

Member of the
Evangelical Christian
Publishers Association

Printed in the United States of America.

*Cast all your anxiety on him
because he cares for you.*

1 PETER 5:7 NIV

Prayer doesn't miraculously take away life's challenges. It's not a magic formula that whisks our troubles away. Jesus Himself prayed to be delivered from the cross—and yet through prayer, He also accepted that this was God's will for Him. The apostle Paul prayed to be delivered from "his thorn of the flesh,"—but when God did not remove this trouble from his life, Paul allowed God to use it to make him stronger. Prayer was the way both Jesus and Paul struggled with their emotional reactions to life's difficulties. It allowed them to transform the meaning of their circumstances, so that what had been a crisis became an opportunity for God's creative work.

Prayer can do the same for us. As it opens us up to God's Spirit, we will see Him working through us and in us. Prayer will bring us peace even in the midst of the most difficult times.

Use these encouraging prayer starters as jumping-off points for your own prayers. Many of them are based on scripture. All of them can be used as "conversation starters" between your heart and God's!

1

Everything I'm Feeling

❧

Jesus, I need Your help. It's hard to even describe everything I'm feeling. I'm overwhelmed, disappointed, exhausted, and anxious, but I give it all to You. Thank You that You are at God's right hand right now, interceding for me in prayer (Hebrews 7:25). Give me Your grace, and help me to extend it to others, especially to those who are part of the issues I'm facing.

2
Litigation

Father, the pressure and uncertainty of this lawsuit is crushing my spirit and sickening my body. I am trying to represent You as I face it, but I believe the suit has no legal merit. Please get it dismissed in whatever way You choose. You are my strength and my shield (Psalm 28:7), and You have said that no weapon formed against me shall succeed (Isaiah 54:17).

3
Comfort in Affliction

❦

Blessed be You, God, the Father of my Lord Jesus Christ, for You are the Father of mercies and the God of all comfort. You comfort me in all my affliction, including this depression that has me in its grip. Use me one day to comfort those who are going through something similar. May I pass along the comfort You give to me now (2 Corinthians 1:3–4).

4

Patiently Waiting

⤜⤚

I'm waiting patiently for You, Lord. I know You will lean down to me and hear my cry. You will draw me up out of the pit of destruction, this miry bog of depression where I'm stuck. You will set my feet on the rock, and You will make my steps steady. And then You will put a new song in my mouth, a song of praise to God. Many will see what You have done for me, and they too will put their trust in You (Psalm 40:1–3).

5
Out of the Pit

I've been here before, God. Depressed. I know that last time there came a brighter day. You lifted me out of the pit. You took away the veil and revealed joy again. . .slowly at first, and then one day I could hardly remember the depressed state I had walked in for so long. Bless me with recovery again. Heal my mind and heart, I pray.

6
When I Fail

I want to be successful. Who doesn't? I want to do well in my career and climb the ladder. I want to be a good friend and coworker. And yet, I fail. I let people down. I miss deadlines. I come up short. Remind me that You love me not one bit less when I fail than when I am victorious. Thank You for Your unconditional love, God.

7

Financial Perspective

❧

Jesus, protect my heart against serving myself with my money instead of You. You made it clear that You expect a return on Your investment in us (Luke 19)—which shows that money can be used to make a profit without greed. I want to use what You give me to bless my family and my community, to bring people into Your kingdom, and to make my finances part of my witness for Your glory.

8
Change for Good

~~

Creator God, I focus so often on how I want others to change. I pray for them, I nag them, I lecture them, I beg them, I try to manipulate them. Ultimately, none of it does much good. Instead, God, show me where *I* need to change. I put myself into Your hands. I'm willing to have You do whatever it takes to heal my relationships.

9

He Is Enough

❧

Lord, I'm realizing that when I reach the point where I have nothing left but You, I can finally realize that You alone are enough. All my questions won't be answered in this life. My circumstances may not be improved. I'll have to let go of some of the things I've set my heart on. But none of that matters. You are the strength of my heart and my portion forever.

10
Self-Care

Remind me, heavenly Father, even in the midst of my grief to take care of myself. It's hard to care right now. Nothing seems to matter very much. But I know others need me—You need me—and *I* need me (as funny as that sounds). Help me to take time to eat healthy meals. Give me the gift of sleep and relaxation. Remind me to exercise, even if it's just going for a walk.

11
He Is Here

You are my refuge and strength, God, my ever-present help in the midst of challenges. Therefore, I won't be scared—even if the earth gives way beneath my feet, even if the mountains fall into the oceans (Psalm 46:1–3). In the midst of all these challenges, I know You are with me.

12

When Death Comes

❦

You died, Jesus. You died upon the cross. You died, just as I am dying here in this place now. You took a final breath, just as I will soon. But hallelujah, You did not stay in the grave! Because of Your death, my sin was forgiven and I was made right with God. Thank You for dying for me that I might have eternal life.

13

The Roller Coaster of Grief

❧

Grief is like a roller coaster, Father, and I'm so tired of riding. I want to forget. I want to get off this tumultuous, up-and-down cycle. And yet, I know that shutting down my emotions is not healthy. I must ride this out. Will You come with me? Will You sit beside me so I can cling to You when I'm afraid? I need You, Father, as I ride out this deep period of grief.

14
Hope above All

Today I pray that each time I begin to dwell on what I *can't* do, Lord, You will bring to mind something that I *can*. I'm still able to do many things even though I'm ill. I can pray. I can encourage someone over the phone. I can do some things even though I'm not able to leave my home. Replace my negative thoughts with hopeful, positive ones. I can. I can. I can.

15
Struggling to Believe

∽

God, forgive me for doubting You. I don't want to be like Thomas who demanded tangible proof. He wanted to see the nail scars in Your hands before he would believe You. I find myself feeling like that at times—wishing You could come down here and chat with me for a while, assuring me You have my future under control. Your Word gives me all the promises I need. I know that. I want to believe. Help my unbelief (Mark 9:23–24).

16

Celebrating with Others

Lord, You know the desires of my heart. Help me to be happy for others when they are successful or receive blessings or rewards. Just because all of the longings in my own life are not yet fulfilled, I don't want to be bitter about others' victories. Help me, Father, as I struggle with jealousy.

17

Trust over Worry

Lord, I'm a worrier. I worry about my family and my friends. I worry about the future because there are so many unknowns. I know that in my anxiety I sin because I'm not trusting You. Please replace my fear with faith. Please help me to rely on You when I begin to worry needlessly.

18
Peaceful Sleep

❧

Father, I need Your peace to guard my heart and mind (Philippians 4:7). I need You to help control my emotions. They spin out of control when I'm tired. Help me to sleep. Restful sleep makes such a difference in my ability to face daily trials. I'm a better person when I get my sleep. Please allow me to find peace and to sleep well tonight when my head hits the pillow.

19
The Armor of God

❧

Lord, make me strong in Your might. Help me to put on Your entire armor, so that I can resist the devil's schemes. I know that ultimately, this is a spiritual situation. I'm not dealing with flesh and blood who want to hurt me, but rather the spiritual forces of evil. Let me clasp the shield of faith, so that I can stand firm, even now. Armor me in truth and righteousness (Ephesians 6:10–18).

20
Generosity

❧

Jesus, let me not be so preoccupied with my own financial problems that I forget that others are in need. You told us in Your Word that it is more blessed to give than to receive, so may I never forget to give. Even now, when I have no money to share with others, show me that I still have much to give. Let me be generous with my time and energy; show me ways I can reach out and be of use to others.

21
How Can I Forgive?

God, I stayed true to my spouse—but my spouse was unfaithful to me. How can I forgive? How can I ever trust again? How can I even try to rebuild this broken marriage? Lord, give me wisdom to face the future. Show me Your way. Heal my heart.

22
A Loved One's Addiction

❧

I can't change the people I love, God, no matter how much I love them. Only You can do that. You know how this addiction in my loved one's life hurts me, how much I wish I could do something, how helpless I feel. I give my feelings to You. I give my loved one to You. I give this entire situation to You. I trust You to bring Your healing power to my loved one's life.

23
Confidently Forgiven

I am so ashamed of my sin, Lord. It's always before me. Please remind me that when I ask You to forgive me, You are faithful to do so. I don't have to walk away hanging my head. I can stand tall. I am made righteous through my Savior's death on the cross for me. My sin is forgiven, and I can walk with confidence as a child of the living God.

24
Who I Am on the Inside

God, You don't look at the outward appearance but at the heart. You are not concerned with my height or weight. You don't see as men see. You see who I am on the inside. Remind me that my heart is what matters most. Thank You for loving me the way You do, Lord.

25
When My Words Aren't Honoring God

⤜⤛

May the words of my mouth be pleasing to You. I struggle with this. When I'm tired and stressed, I often fail to speak to others in a way that honors You, God. Help me to take a deep breath in those times and whisper a prayer. Help me to remember that my tongue has the power to lift others up or tear them down. I want to honor You with how I speak in every situation.

26
Greed Disguised as Good

❧

Lord, my greed has disguised itself as good, but everything I get leaves me feeling unsatisfied—and I realize that's not Your best for me. I've found myself thinking, *I deserve that* or *If I don't get this, I'll be missing out.* Forgive me for thinking of You as my genie instead of my God. I want to honor You by representing You well in every part of my life, especially my finances.

27

The Trap of Angry Words

❧

Father, I'm trying to think of a time when I won someone over by using angry, harsh words during an argument. And I can't. I may have made my point, but I lost trust—and a chance to honor You. Forgive me for all the times I've tried to defend myself or You unnecessarily, or put a principle ahead of a person, or righteousness ahead of relationship. Let my offenses be limited to the truth of the Gospel.

28
Forgiving Family Offenses

∿

God, help me to place You above my family. Family is important, but I know that You are more important still. When I cease to find my worth in what my relatives think of me, perhaps I'll be freed up to love them and forgive them for the ways they've hurt me. Help me to find my identity in You.

29
Jesus Understands My Pain

❦

Jesus, You were fully man even as You were fully God. You came to earth and lived life as one of us. I can turn to You even when no one else is around, even when no one understands. You experienced great pain. You hung on the cross and gave Your very life for me. You died a painful death. Thank You for being my Savior and Friend. Thank You for being there for me every day and for walking with me through this pain.

30
Remembering His Help

⤜⤛

Heavenly Father, I look back and I see the pain but also Your provision. I see the way You took me out of yesterday and brought me into today, Father. In the Bible, Your people built altars as reminders. I call to mind in this moment the ways in which You have rescued me. I thank You for the people who have helped me. I read in Your Word of Your great love for me. Continue to heal my heart, I pray, in ways that only You can.

31
Contentment and Discontentment

Circumstances dictate my level of contentment. It shouldn't be that way but honestly, it is. When good things happen, I'm a happy Christian, praising You in church and singing and praying throughout the week. When hard times come, I blame You. I ask where You are. I turn away. Funny how when I come back around, You are always there. You haven't moved. I'm the fickle one. Create in me a more content spirit that I might be faithful to You regardless of my situation or my station in life.

32

He Is Always Near

You will not leave me. You have called me by name. You call me Your own. When I pass through deep waters, You will not let me drown (Isaiah 43:1–5). Loneliness overwhelms me, but You are still here with me. You never look away. You never wander. You are my God, always near. For that I am so very thankful.

33
Prodigal Children

Jesus, You told the story of the prodigal son. I imagine the father holding his tongue, fighting the urge to tell his son what a terrible mistake he was making. He let him go. Give me the grace to let my children go their own way. They're adults now and must make their own decisions.

34
Facing the Lions

God, You showed up for Daniel in the lions' den. You have proven time and time again in my own life that You always come through for Your children. You know what we need and when we need it. This life is a journey, and it's a lesson in trust. Help me to be a scholar who learns the lessons early so that I am not worrying my years away.

35
Make Me Whole

❦

Lord, I know I am precious in Your eyes. I am beautiful and spotless in Your sight. Help me to hold my head high, wrapped in the knowledge that I am Your child. Take away my shame. Heal my wounded memories. Create something new inside me. I trust You to do that which seems impossible. Make me whole again, I pray.

36
Making Peace

I want to bear fruit for You in this world, Father. I know that without spending time in prayer daily, I lose sight of my purpose on earth. I'm to bring glory to You and to lead others to know You as their personal Savior. How can I do this if I'm constantly at odds with those around me? Help me to love those whom You have placed in my circles of influence. I want to be known as a peacemaker.

37
Missing a Parent

Father, I'm thankful for the memories, but they bring me little comfort today. Instead, they hurt. I miss my parent. I miss all the happy times. I pray that one day I'll be able to enjoy the memories again without the pain. Bring me through grief to the other side, I pray.

38
Debt

God, I give You my finances. I should have done so a long time ago. I thought I had the money under control, but I didn't. It began to get away from me little by little, and here I am in debt that's swallowing up not only me but my family with me. Forgive me and help me, God. I give it all to You, and I ask that You help me to sort it out and to do better with financial responsibility in the future. I want our family to honor You in every area—our finances included.

39
Even If...

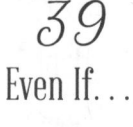

God, I know there is one thing that will never change. You will never leave me. Even if my job changes. . .even if I must move across the country. . .even if I'm abandoned by others. . .even if I grow ill or disabled and cannot live the way I'm used to. . .You will be there. You will never leave me or forsake me (Deuteronomy 31:8). I take great comfort in Your faithfulness and loyalty, heavenly Father.

40
A Good Night's Rest

Dear God, I want to lie down and sleep in peace. I want to believe that You will keep me safe (Psalm 4:8). Above all, I want to just close my eyes and fall asleep. It's a goal that seems unattainable to me even though it comes very naturally for others. Please grant me a good night's rest tonight, I pray.

41
I Wish. . .

❧

I'm deeply sorry for the way things turned out. I wish I could turn back the hands of time and change my actions and hold my tongue. I wish I could make different choices. I wish. . .but wishing can go on and on, and still nothing changes. I heard it said once that if we spend too much time dwelling on the past, we will miss the present and have no future. I don't want that to be me, God! Help me to release the past and take hold of the future that You have in store for me. I want to be used in a mighty way for Your kingdom.

42
Confident in Christ

God, I want to trade my low self-esteem for Christ-esteem. Make me confident in who I am through Christ. I wrestle with dark spiritual powers of evil, but You are greater than these (Ephesians 6:12). Remind me of my salvation and of my great worth in Christ Jesus.

43
Working through Conflicts

God, remind me that my sun should not go down on my anger. Help me not to go to bed nursing a grudge that will haunt my sleep and get up with me in the morning. Instead, let me value my relationships enough that I commit myself to working through the conflicts that arise. I know You want us to live in harmony.

44

Dependent on God's Love

When everything is going well, I'm not as anxious, Lord. I feel like I'm in control. My sense of security is stable. But when I feel threatened or overwhelmed, I start to get anxious. Use my anxiety, Lord, to remind me that I'm dependent on Your love. Let each nagging fear be a nudge that turns me toward You and Your strength.

45

Heal My Broken Heart

Jesus, I know You came to heal the brokenhearted. Heal my broken heart, I pray. You came to deliver captives into freedom. Set me free from abuse. You came to heal those who are bruised. I ask that You heal the scars of abuse in my heart, in my mind and memories, and in my life. Please rescue me!

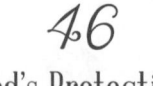

46
God's Protection

Lord, like a mother hen protecting her chicks, You protect Your children (Psalm 91:4). I have no reason to worry or fear. You are always with me, watching over me, and laying out the path before me one step at a time. You make a way for me to handle anything You ask me to. You created me and You know me better than I even know myself. I trust You, God.

47
Taking Responsibility

~

God, some of this is not my fault. Help me to see the parts I do need to take responsibility for and make the necessary changes. I want this relationship to be better, and yet I keep doing and saying the same things. Wanting is not enough. I must take action. Guide me, I pray, and help me to see my part in it all so that I can change it.

48
He Knows Me

∞

I am fully known. You put me together in my mother's womb. But I have walked through this life with only a glimpse of who You are. My humanity has kept me from knowing fully. There are secret things that simply cannot be understood in this life. I'm coming close to the time when I will know! I will know fully just as I am fully known. I look forward to that, Lord (1 Corinthians 13:12)!

49
The Weight of Sorrow

Give me a glad heart, Lord Jesus. A glad heart makes a cheerful face. I've been weighed down far too long with sorrow. My spirit has been crushed by this deep regret over what I've done. I long to be happy once again (Proverbs 15:13).

50
Asking God to Take Over

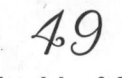

Today I pray that You will go before me. In every moment of weakness, I pray You will show up to provide supernatural strength. Where I am failing, bring success. Where I am losing my grip, take hold. Where I am discouraged, lift me up. I will trust in You.

51
Growing Closer to God

∽

I remember learning in school that the brain must experience challenge or it will stop growing new dendrites. I suppose the spiritual life is like this as well. I tend to grow closer to You during times of trials. When life is just moving along normally, I often drift from You. When I face a challenge, I run to Your side. I'm more faithful in prayer. I seek You in Your Word, and I walk closer to Your side. Challenges can really be a positive thing in my life!

52
Refocus on Him

I come before You, Lord, and I admit I'm not in a very good state. I'm stressed out and overworked and tired, so tired. It's in moments such as these that I refocus. I find You there. You never moved. It was I who drifted. I look up and find my Father's face smiling down at me. You offer me an easy yoke. I accept, Abba Father. I will rest in You.

53
Loneliness

God, I'm lonely. There are so many things I want to do, but often, I can't think of anyone who would want to go and do them with me. I long for a close friend. Please help me to find a new Christian friend. Remind me, oh Father, that even if I have hundreds of friends, I need You more than any other.

54

Praying for Enemies

❧

Jesus, help me to fight evil with good. Give me the strength to take a deep breath and show love even to those who are not easy to love. I read about how You asked the Father to forgive those who crucified You. That's unbelievable to me, and yet, I'm called to love and pray for my enemies as well. Help me, I pray.

55
The Sting of Betrayal

❧

I sit here hurting in disbelief. Betrayal stings. You know the sting of betrayal. You were betrayed by Peter three times before the cock crowed. He said he would never turn away from You and yet, it happened. Remind me that in our humanity we are weak. Give me a forgiving spirit that I might reach a place where I can forgive those who have betrayed me.

56
Bitterness

Lord, I'm bitter about a situation. You know all the players and the plot of the story. You know the details before I even spill them out before You. Please calm my spirit and give me the ability to let it go. I'm hurting myself more than anyone else when I hold on to this and stew about it day and night.

57
Praying for My Wayward Child

❧

This child is Yours, God. You blessed me with her and I gave her back to You. I trusted You with her all these years. Why would I try to take her back now? You know my daughter better than I do, better than she even knows herself. Please protect her. Please lead her back to the right path.

58
Life's Demands

❧

I'm so overwhelmed by all of life's demands on me. Before I begin my work, I'll stop and spend time with You. I choose to put You first. I choose to rest in You so that You will bless the labor of my hands. I need You, God.

59
A Hard Move

Help me to be positive about this move, Lord. Even though the circumstances are not ideal, help me to trust You. I need to be strong for others who are looking to me for their own strength in this move, God. Please give me a smile and a countenance that displays confidence that can come only from You.

60
Loss of a Relationship

❧

I need You, God. I can't walk through this alone. I'm grieving for one who still lives. It's harder, I think, than grieving for the dead. This person is not part of my life anymore, but this is not my choice. I simply must accept the decision another has made and walk through the grief that is the result. I can't control all of the losses in my life. Walk with me, God. We can do this together. I can do it if You stay with me and assure me that You will never leave.

61
The Deepest of Hurts

❧

Jesus, my own family has hurt me so deeply. I don't feel like forgiving, but I know it's Your command. I know that I should forgive seventy times seven times. I know that I cannot be healed unless this war within my family comes to a halt. Please guide me in how to help that happen. It needs to happen soon, Lord.

62
When My Attitude Won't Change

~

God, I know that contentment begins with an attitude change. I haven't been able to make it. I see glimpses of it at times, but my overall outlook is bleak, not sunny. I need to find a place of contentment. Show me the way. It seems so overwhelming, so out of reach. Show me just a small step that I can take today to become more content.

63
Walk with Me, Lord

❧

Heavenly Father, the challenges I face are not unique to me. There's nothing strange about facing trials and hardships. Believers have walked through rough situations for generations. I should not be shocked when a challenge comes my way (1 Peter 4:12). Just as You have stood with Christ followers of the past, stand with me now, I pray. Walk with me, Lord. Carry me. I need Your help.

64
Waiting for Understanding

Jesus, You healed the sick. You caused the lame to walk. You took away the lepers' spots. I don't understand why You won't heal me in the same way. I know that there are things we just won't understand until we get to heaven. Please comfort me as I wait to understand Your ways.

65
Praying for My Elderly Parents

Father, I pray that You will give my parents bright spots today. Even as their bodies are beginning to fail them, I know that You remain faithful and true. Give them neighbors who care and joyful moments such as watching birds out their kitchen window, just little things to cheer them through the day. Thank You, Lord, for loving my mom and dad.

66
Carry Me Today, Lord

❧

God, these are hard days. I wake up to the sun shining through my window, and I wonder how it could be so bright and pretty outside when I feel so sad and sick inside. I know that it may take time, but I pray that You will restore in my heart a sense of joy. And for today, Lord, will You carry me? Will You please remind me that You are so very close and that You have not—and will not *ever*—let me go?

67
The Voice of the Shepherd

I know the voice of my Shepherd. I have been listening to it for many years. I am being called upon in a way I never knew possible to tune into that voice and seek direction only from the One who knows me best. Give me grace for the moment and the healing and power to get through this, Lord.

68
The Price of Love

❧

God, I know this grief is the price I pay for having loved with all my heart. I don't regret loving my child with the love only a parent can give. I would do it all again even if I knew it was going to end. I would love just the same. I would pour out myself the same way. How I miss the privilege of raising my child. Hold me, Father, as I mourn this deep, deep loss.

69
Remembering My Parent

❦

Dear God, I am who I am largely because of my parent, and now I am without this vital person in my life. Help me to remember all the lessons I learned just through doing life together with my parent for many years. Help me to forget the bad and to hold on to the good. Help me to honor my parent's memory by being a beautiful legacy as their child in this world.

70
Please Change What I Cannot

I wish that I could wave a magic wand and cause the one I love to walk away from this addiction. I feel like I have to compete with it day and night. I can't change the situation, but I can bring it to You in prayer. I put this whole thing into Your strong and capable hands, heavenly Father. I ask that You change what I cannot.

71

Trusting in Everything

❧

God, help me to build my house upon the Rock of Christ Jesus, not on shifting sands. I know that there is no stability in doubting. I want my hope to be steadfast and true. You are the Alpha and the Omega, the beginning and the end. Help me to trust You with these and with everything in between.

72
Seeking Contentment

Help me to be content with much or with little. My bank account does not define who I am or the degree of happiness in my life. Whether I find myself wealthy or poor, help me to honor You and to be thankful to You for what I have (Philippians 4:11–13, 19).

73
Salt and Light

❧

God, You have called me to be salt and light to Your world. When I'm abusing drugs, I can't be either of these. I want my conversations to be seasoned with fervor for You. I want to shine as a light for You in the dark places of this world. I could even help others to get off drugs. Please continue to keep me sober so that I can be salt and light, I pray.

74
Bring Me Counsel

I feel like I need some help, Lord. I don't think I can move past this without assistance. If there's a certain friend or counselor I should turn to, please put that person in my path. Make it clear to me, I pray, if I should attend a support group. I want to heal, Father, and I need help.

75
You Gather My Tears

❦

I know that You never miss a tear that falls down my face, Lord. You gather my tears. You hear my cries for relief. One day there will be no more tears. One day I will run and dance and enjoy a new, flawless body. I will spend eternity in heaven with You. For now, remind me that You are near. Touch my weary brow. Restore my hope, I pray.

76
Slow to Anger

❧

Lord, I know that the tongue can be a positive or a negative. Help me to use my words to bring You honor and glory rather than cause petty arguments. You take no pleasure in hearing Your children squabble with one another over issues that really don't matter in the long run. Help me to be more like Jesus. Help me to be slow to anger.

77
I Am Not Helpless

❧

Jesus, release me from these feelings of helplessness. I want to be the person You've called me to be, and I want to live under Your authority just as You lived under the Father's while You were on earth. Forgive me for any lack of obedience, for any desire to choose my way over Yours, so that I can fulfill Your promise that "whoever believes in me will do the works I have been doing, and they will do even greater things than these" (John 14:12 NIV).

78
He Is Right on Time

Like Mary and Martha who waited for You to come and heal Lazarus, my jaw drops when You don't show up to rescue me or provide what I desire. Remind me that You are never early or late but always right on time. What feels like a disappointment is only a detour that will take me to something greater.

79
Turning Bad into Good

❧

God, in Your Word it seems like You are always turning bad things into good things. You struck down Saul on the road to Damascus only to raise him up as a great leader. You brought a flood, but when it was over, You made the world into a better place. Use this pain, this difficult time. Create a new thing here, and cause me to see and appreciate it.

80
Sing a New Song

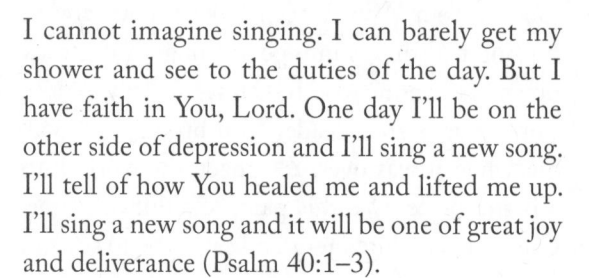

I cannot imagine singing. I can barely get my shower and see to the duties of the day. But I have faith in You, Lord. One day I'll be on the other side of depression and I'll sing a new song. I'll tell of how You healed me and lifted me up. I'll sing a new song and it will be one of great joy and deliverance (Psalm 40:1–3).

81
Not Getting My Way

❧

Remind me, God, that You are the giver of all good gifts. You don't withhold any good gift from Your children whom You love. Sometimes I feel like You're not giving me what I want or need. I grow angry with You even though I feel terribly guilty about that anger. Please forgive me and show me how to trust You even when I'm not getting my way.

82
Healthy Boundaries

✦

Heavenly Father, I hear about boundaries, but I don't even know what they would look like in my world. I'm constantly doing everything for everyone, trying to please, trying to keep the peace. I know this isn't healthy. Teach me where I need to establish healthy boundaries, Father. Give me the opportunity to take care of myself so that I can have something left over to give to others.

83
When I Fail

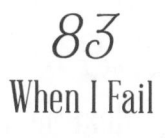

My failure leads me to repentance. I come to You when I fail. I seek You. When You say You work all things together for good for those who love You, I think that includes our failures. If I were always a winner, I would not rely on You as much. I fall into Your arms when I fail. You are always there, steadfast and true.

84
Heal Me

Father, You healed the blind and the lame and even those with leprosy. I know that You can heal me, too. I didn't see myself as sick for a long time, but now I am beginning to. This is an illness. I need Your divine intervention. I need You to show up as the Great Physician in my life.

85
Hurt People Hurt People

❧

Heavenly Father, I pray right now in this moment for the ones who have hurt me. I lift them up by name before Your throne. Perhaps they truly "know not what they do." I know that hurt people are known to hurt people. Please heal the wounds in their souls. Please use me as a representative of Your grace and generosity.

86
A Time for Everything

～～

There is a time for everything and a purpose for everything that happens (Ecclesiastes 3:1). I know this change is not a surprise to You, Lord. You see all the pieces of the puzzle that make up my life. I can only see one piece at a time. You see how this "new normal" is going to draw me closer to You and how it will challenge and shape me. Please allow this change in my life to bring You glory, just as everything should. I love You, Lord.

87
God Is on My Side

I know You are on my side, Lord. You want me to be whole. You want me to trust You so that I can receive Your blessings. You want to give me the capacity to walk in Your grace and wrap myself in Your love. You are the Creator of the world. There is nothing too hard for You!

88
Hurt and Mistreated

❧

Jesus, someone did me wrong. You saw it. You were there. Why shouldn't I hold a grudge? I've been hurt and mistreated. You understand, You say? You too were wronged. You were treated unjustly. Your heart did not grow hard even when the soldiers put bitter vinegar to Your parched lips as You hung dying on the cross. You asked the Father to forgive them. Grant me just a tiny bit of that strength, Savior, that I might forgive those who have acted unfairly toward me.

89
Jesus to Others

Remind me, Father, that I may be the only Jesus some will ever see. Please help me to be a loving example of what it means to be a Christian. I see Christians arguing the cause of Christ in such an angry, bitter manner. I don't believe this is how You want us to do it. In fact, I know it isn't.

90
You Follow after Me

❧

The psalmist wrote that You go before me on my path—and You follow after me. That means You were waiting for me there in the middle of what looked to me like such a terrible accident—and now that it's over, You're here with me still, helping me to pick up the pieces. Help me be willing to build something new in the wake of this disaster, with Your help.

91
Disappointment

God, I'm not the only one to be disappointed. When I look at the Bible, I see person after person who hoped for something—and then was disappointed. Abraham, Moses, David, the prophets, they all learned that disappointment is only temporary. What looks like a loss from my perspective now will one day be revealed as only the next step toward the amazing thing You were doing all along.

92
Grief that Persists

Time goes by, Lord, but my grief is still here. I know that others no longer know how to help me. They want me to be done with this grieving process. They want me to move on and be the person I used to be. But I'm not done with grieving. I will never be done with grieving for my child. I cannot move on, because to do so would mean to leave my child behind. I will never again be the person I once was. I can't be. But Lord, I know You still have a purpose for me. Please reveal that purpose to me. Use this grief to transform me into a new instrument of Your love. May my life be a living memorial to my child. Even more, may it be what You want it to be. Give me strength to place my grief in Your hands.

93
Endurance to Strength

❦

Jesus, I don't know how to obey the apostle Paul when he tells us to rejoice in our sufferings. I will wait on You, though, believing that somehow this suffering will produce endurance. . .and endurance will produce strength of character. . .and that hope will grow out of that, a hope that will never be disappointed. Thank You for pouring Your love into my heart through the Holy Spirit (Romans 5:3–5).

94
Part of God's Plan

〜

Father, I know that there is a time for everything. Your Word tells me this. I don't understand how this could be part of Your plan, but I pray You will use even this for Your glory. May I look back one day in the future and see how Your hand was at work in my life even though it was a very difficult time.

95
True Surrender

When I'm anxious, I pray that You will remind me that I must cast my cares on You, Jesus. You ask me to do this. You tell me to cast them. That means rid myself of them. That means throw them with all my might at Your feet. Help me to truly surrender to You, Lord.

96
Betrayal of a Friend

❧

Lord, I betrayed my friend. I shared information that was not to be shared. I have not been trustworthy. Whether my friend knows or not doesn't matter. I feel so guilty inside. Please forgive me for being a gossip. In the moment, it feels good to be the one in the know. Afterward, it saddens me that I was not true to my friend. "A gossip betrays a confidence, but a trustworthy person keeps a secret" (Proverbs 11:13).

97
The Shadow of Death

The valley of the shadow of death never seemed so real as it does today. I will not fear it. You are here with me, just as You promised to be. You protect me. You comfort me. I will live forever in the house of my Lord (Psalm 23).

98
Seek out the Lonely

Help me, Lord, to reach out to those who may be lonely today. It often helps me to do something for others. There is always someone worse off than me, someone I can minister to, someone who could use a friend. Show me the opportunities You have for me to be a light today.

99
Making Decisions for My Parents

❧

Father, it's not always easy to know what to do. I want my parents to enjoy independence as long as they possibly can. But I'm scared when things happen that could prove unsafe for them. As I make tough decisions for my elderly parents, please guide me and give me wisdom.

100
Fighting the Right Battle

❧

I think about young David with his slingshot. He was able to kill the giant not because of his own strength or expertise but because his confidence was in You, God. He was fighting the right battle. He was on the right side. Draw me close to You. I don't want to be on the front lines in this battle without You at my side as my commanding officer.

101
Taking Care of Myself

❧

Lord, thank You for reminding me through friends and loved ones to take care of myself. Others need me. You need me. I cannot lose myself completely in this. I must rely on You to see me through just as You've seen me through other seasons of difficulty. This seems too big, but nothing is too big for my God.

102
Toward Completeness

❧

Jesus, this test feels more like a dead end than just a bump in the road. I'm so disappointed. Yet I know that this trial will strengthen my faith and instill perseverance in me, helping me toward completeness (James 1:2–4). Please use even the disappointments in my life to make me more like You.

103
Facing Surgery

❧

Lord, my loved one is facing surgery. Be his peace right now as You strengthen his body and prepare his mind and spirit. Give his doctors the greatest skill possible and guide the outcome toward the highest possible good. Would You help him to recover quickly and be better off because of this operation? Thank You, Lord, for my dear one. I lift him up to You in Jesus' name.

104
Resolving Conflicts

~

God, You want Your children to live at peace with one another. You tell us never to let the sun go down on our anger. I find myself stewing about a situation when I go to sleep and then picking right up where I left off the next day as soon as I wake. I know this is not Your will for me. Help me to value my relationships more and to resolve conflicts quickly.

105
No Fear

God, You are my refuge and strength, an ever-present help in trouble (Psalm 46:1–2). Because of this, I choose not to fear, regardless of what happens. Even the worst situations will not cause me to crumble. You are in control. You will work all things together for my good.

106
Strengthen My Family

❧

Family is such a gift. Help us to remember that throughout the year, not just on special occasions like birthdays and Christmas. Help us to be kinder to one another, God. I don't want to look back in years to come and see a family torn apart by daily stresses. I want our family to be strong. Help me to do what I should do as the woman of this home to help make us a strong family again.

107
The First to Apologize

❧

Proverbs warns against stirring up anger. It says that this will bring nothing but trouble. Please help me to have the strength to walk away from arguments, Lord. I'm imperfect, and I will fail at this sometimes. Give me then the wisdom and patience to deal with the outcome. Give me the humility to be the first to apologize and to make amends.

108
Beauty from Ashes

Lord, You saw Paul when You looked at Saul. You bring beauty from ashes. Sometimes I wonder how You could love me. I don't even love myself at times. Help me this day to see the lies others have told me about myself as what they are—lies. Remind me of the truth that I am fearfully and wonderfully made in Your image and that You have great plans for my future.

109
Faith in the Intangible

❧

Father, I want to have faith like the men and women I read about in the Bible. Often, I trust only in what I can see before me. I realize that You call me to faith in that which I have not yet seen (Hebrews 11:1). It's really not faith if I only believe in the tangible. I must trust in the intangible. All around me there is proof that You exist. Help me to count my blessings and to construct altars along the way so that I can remember times You came through for me (Genesis 35:3).

110
Work as You Choose, Lord

❧

God, teach me about prayer through this illness. I know You do not always choose to answer prayers as we might want. I know that our perspectives are often too limited for us to even understand what we truly need most. And yet I believe You always hear my prayers. You never ignore me. My prayers always connect me to You—and they open up a space where You can work in me. Please work in me, Lord. In whatever way You choose. This is my prayer.

111
I'm Angry and Hurt

❧

God, I've struggled to forgive certain people. I've made all sorts of justifications for not doing so, but in the end, I'm just angry and hurt. I can feel my pain growing in me like a weed, though, and I need Your help to root it out. I know that starts with me forgiving those who have hurt me. I'm sorry for forgetting all You have forgiven me for. Forgiveness is based on Your character and the redeeming work of Christ at the Cross. I leave my anger and pain there. Fill the void with Your grace, mercy, and forgiveness, so I can extend to others what You first gave me.

112
Special Days

❧

Oh God, I can't face the calendar anymore. Anniversaries, Valentine's Day, birthdays, Christmas
. . .they all bring memories and fresh pain. I miss
my spouse in new ways with the passing of the
seasons. I can't help but think, *Last year at this
time, we were. . .* And I resent the passage of time,
because each day takes me further away from the
days I shared with my spouse. Lord, I give my
days to You. May I seek You in each one, even
the ones that are most painful.

113
Love at All Times

God, Your Word emphasizes love over and over again. In 1 Corinthians, we read that it's even greater than hope and peace. Please help me to show love to others. I don't want to have an argumentative spirit. Please help me to be kind and loving at all times, even when things don't go my way.

114
I Am Always Loved

You are a good, good Father, and I am loved by You. When I'm afraid of others or of circumstances, remind me of Your goodness. When I feel I cannot face the future, remind me that I am Your beloved child. You are always good, and I am always loved. I am going to be just fine.

115
The Battle Is the Lord's

~

I love the verse in scripture that says the battle is the Lord's. My battle is not with weapons or against a large army, but it feels every bit as challenging! I fight a battle to love myself and to forgive the ones who have hurt me. I fight it every day. I'm thankful that the battle is Yours, Jesus. I can't do it on my own.

116
Defined by My Illness

～

Heavenly Father, this illness has begun to define me. I want my identity to be in Jesus Christ and not in my sickness. Please remind me that I am a cherished child of the King, saved by grace through faith in the Messiah. I'm not just a homebound sick person. I will not let Satan convince me that I'm just a burden and that others would be better off if I were not here. I have value and worth because I am part of the family of God.

117
Wasted Money

God, I have not been wise with my money. You know that I have wasted money on things that did not honor You. Help me to make better choices as I move forward. I want to do better and to honor You with my spending. You are the giver of all good gifts. Give me the self-control to use my money in ways that will further Your kingdom and not be wasted on things of the world.

118
Worn Out

~~~

God, I am worn out. So many things have been happening that require my care and attention, but somehow I let my busyness push my need for You out of the picture. It's no wonder I'm so frustrated and weak. But here I am, snapping out of it. I need You, Lord. Your grace is enough for me. I know You will give me what I need—the rest, the wisdom, the will—to keep seeking You as life rolls on.

119
I Grow with Each New Test

❧

You are the Lord of the Universe. You created worlds from nothing. You formed me within my mother's womb and brought me into being. You have been with me, in every challenge I have ever faced, since I was born. With each new test, I've grown. You've revealed Yourself in new ways all through my life. I'm waiting now to see what You will do next!

120
The Death of Hopes

I'm grieving today, Lord—grieving for the loss of companionship in my life, for the death of hopes, for broken promises, and for plans that will never be fulfilled. The pain I feel scares me. I'm afraid I can never recover from this wound. Give me courage to mourn my marriage. Give me strength to place it in Your loving hands and leave it there. Give me hope again. Heal my heart, I pray.

121
I Still Have Doubts

God, You know I still have doubts. But despite my doubts, I affirm that neither life nor death, neither angels nor any spiritual power, neither height nor depth, nothing the future holds—in fact, nothing whatsoever will ever be able to separate me from Your love (Romans 8:38–39)!

122
Dealing with Dishonesty

❦

Loving Lord, I hate to admit this, but being honest isn't always easy for me. Little lies slip out of my mouth so glibly. I don't even think about them ahead of time. I tell myself they don't matter. After all, I'm not lying about *big* things. I'm only lying about trivial things, to make my life easier, to smooth over awkwardness, to let me have my way without upsetting anyone. Lord Jesus, remind me that You are truth. Teach me that lying hurts Your Spirit. Help me to love the truth.

123
The Lord will Provide

Lord, You are *Jehovah-Jireh* (the Lord will provide). You provided a ram for Abraham to sacrifice in place of his beloved son Isaac. You provided right at the moment that a sacrifice was needed. Thank You for the assurance that You will provide for my needs as well. I can trust You all of my life—in every stage, at every crossroads. I will trust in my Provider.

124
Move on from Regret

If I confess my sins, You are faithful to forgive and cleanse me of all unrighteousness (1 John 1:9). I don't have to live with regret. It's a burden You desire for me to lay down at Your feet. Help me to do just that, God, and give me the strength to move on rather than pick it up again.

125
He Uses Brokenness

～

God, You use broken vessels. You use broken families. The families of the Bible were far from perfect. Find my broken family useful to Your kingdom, God. Cause us to consider how much better our passion would be spent on spreading the Gospel rather than feuding among ourselves. We've been angry for so long that I'm not sure any of us even remember how it all began. Forgive us, God. Change us. Use us, I pray.

126
Moving on from Divorce

❧

God, help me not to be bitter about this divorce.
I know that bitterness can grow up and fester in
my heart and that it has the potential to ruin my
life. I have seen others allow this to happen, and I
don't want to be like them—sitting around talking
about this for years to come. Give me strength to
grieve well and then to move forward well. Thank
You, Father.

127
Strength of Character

Jesus, the apostle Paul tells me to rejoice in suffering. I must believe that somehow this suffering will produce endurance. . .and endurance will produce strength of character. . .and that hope will grow from that, a hope that will never be disappointed. Thank You for filling me with Your Holy Spirit (Romans 5:3–5).

128
Forgiveness One Day at a Time

❧

One day at a time, Lord. Help me to forgive and forget and to simply take one day at a time. Help me to remember that nothing touches my life if it has not first been filtered through Your fingers. If You have allowed me to walk through a trial, there is a reason for it. Please keep me from becoming bitter toward You, my loving and faithful God.

129
An Empathetic God

~

Sometimes, God, it brings me just a bit of comfort to know that You lost Your Son too. You watched Him hang upon a cross and die a terrible death He did not deserve. You gave Him up willingly for us. I can trust You because Your comfort is not just sympathy but empathy. You too have buried a child.

130

God Numbers Our Days

❧

Nothing comes to me that You have not allowed, God. Even this deep loss of my parent was ordained by You. Your Word says You have ordained each day that we live. You number them. My parent lived the exact number of days that You established. That brings me comfort. It reminds me that You are in control and even now, when nothing seems right, You are holding things together and will continue to do so.

131
Fear of Failure

Sometimes I refuse to try because I'm afraid I'll fail. I did this as a child and I thought I would outgrow it, but I haven't. Instead of avoiding a sport or activity, I now avoid bigger things—like relationships and job applications. Give me confidence, Father, and strengthen my spirit so that it's okay even if I do fail.

132
Losing a Friend

I'm grieving the loss of a friendship, Lord. I remember when this friendship was light and fun, a positive thing in my life. But that was a long, long time ago. You have clearly shown me it was time to walk away. I know that ending this relationship was best for me. But it doesn't take away the sadness I feel. It's hard to let go of someone I love.

133
I Am Free!

❧

Thank You, Lord, for not counting my sin against me. Thank You for washing me white as snow through the blood of Jesus. I don't have to hang my head in shame or guilt. Jesus died once and for all. A supernatural stain lifter, He removed my guilt. Hallelujah! I am free.

134
He Has Overcome

❦

This is not my home. This world is full of trouble, including depression. But You, Jesus, have overcome the world. One day I will experience an existence in heaven that does not include the pain of darkness or this sick feeling of hopelessness. That will be a place of great hope. For now, there are troubles. You will walk us through them. I will keep my eyes on You, and one day I will be fully and forever free of these bouts of depression. That will be a glorious day (John 16:33)!

135
The God of the Impossible

❧

When I begin to doubt You, Lord, bring to mind all the times that You have answered my prayers. Sometimes this helps me to remain calm and trust You even in the midst of circumstances that seem impossible. You are the God of the impossible. You are strong and mighty, sovereign and faithful. I trust You, God.

136
Hidden Sin

I come before You with dirty hands and a dirty heart. I know that the wages of sin is death. I feel as if I'm a dead person somehow still walking around among the living. I confess this sin to You, Father. *[Speak the sin or sins you have been hiding from God here.]* I ask You to forgive me in the powerful name of Jesus and set me on a new course for my life.

137
A Fickle Friend

❧

Lord, it hurts to have a fickle friend. Even small betrayals leave wounds. I make plans with this friend, and she continues to break them at the last minute. She doesn't show up. She calls to cancel. Please guide me as to whether I should continue to show grace or perhaps back away a bit from this person. I need friends whom I can count on to be there.

138
The Power of Love

You emphasized a lot of things in Your teachings, Jesus, but the greatest was love. Love is a powerful force capable of changing a heart. Your love changed my heart. Use me, I pray, to be a living example of unconditional love to others today— especially those who are my enemies.

139
God Will Take Care of Me

❧

God, just as You take care of the lilies of the field and the birds of the air, You will take care of me. You know my needs. I don't have to scurry about or worry excessively about money. I simply need to lay this burden down and trust You. You have come through for me before and You will do so this time. I thank You for taking care of me so well (Matthew 6:28–33).

140
Change as Part of God's Plan

You know the plans You have for me, Sovereign God. Your plans are never to hurt me but always to bring me hope. You have a good future in store for me (Jeremiah 29:11). Help me to look at this change as just a part of the plan. Thank You for assuring me that You are still in control even when things seem a bit out of control in my little world.

141
Laying Down Desire

Heavenly Father, I surrender this longing. I lay down the desire. I'm weary from this burden. I'm tired. I can bear this alone no longer. I need You to help me. I need You to calm my spirit and dry my tears. I am sad and frustrated, but even still, I will praise You, my Creator and Sustainer.

142

Bring Me Calm

Sovereign God, my mind is racing. Please slow my thoughts and bring a calm over me. As I lay here in bed, please let my breathing fall in rhythm with Your spirit. Let me sense Your nearness. Bring to my mind all the times You've protected me and blessed me in the past. I know that I have nothing to fear because You watch over me.

143
The Great Physician

You are the great physician, Father. Whether You choose to heal me in this life or wait until I'm in heaven with a brand-new body, I trust You. I know that You will use this area of my life to grow me closer to You. My faith is stronger because I must look to You every day. Draw me close, and remind me that You are my confidence.

144
God Embraces Me

I'm ashamed to come before You. I am so sorry. I can't even lift my face toward heaven. I have not acted as I should. I've brought disgrace to Your holy name. My iniquities have risen above my head, and my guilt has grown to the heavens (Ezra 9:6). And yet, I know that when I lay my shame before You, You reach down to me and embrace me. You call me Your own. You're a good, good Father, and I am loved by You.

145
Enduring Deep Loss

❧

Dearest Lord, I'm grieving a loss that was long ago. It comes back to me at certain seasons of the year. A situation or a phrase can catch me so unaware. I find myself transported back to another time and another place. The loss feels just as deep and the grief just as strong as it was back then. Comfort me with Your Holy Spirit, I pray. This is a deep loss, and I must not try to brush it off as less. I must acknowledge the pain so that You can provide a healing balm to my soul.

146
When Death Is Knocking

God, it's easy to say one doesn't fear death—until it's knocking at the door. I know I am drawing closer and closer to the time when I will take my final breath. Please reassure me that while death is "the final enemy," You have already defeated it! I will live forever with You in heaven.

147
Praying for Open Doors

❦

Thank You, God, that You promise in Your Word that You will never withhold a good and perfect gift from those who walk with You (Psalm 84:11). My emotions are getting the best of me lately. I begin to believe, at times, that You don't want me to be happy. You seem to be keeping me from my dreams! I know that I can trust Your heart, though, and that this is just a lie Satan wants me to believe. Help me to trust that You are in control and that although You have closed these doors, You surely will open the right ones that You are preparing for me.

148
Praying for Trust

❧

God, I feel like I should apologize to You because I don't trust You. You are the Maker of the universe, and You created me. I believe that. I know that even though I only see in part, I am fully known by You. And yet, how is it that I can't seem to trust that You know the plans You have for me? Help me to relax and believe that You have a bright future in store, plans to bring me hope not harm (Jeremiah 29:11).

149

Be My Strength Today

❧

I want to soar as the eagles. I watch them, God. They take flight and so gracefully soar above the earth. I want my spirit to be light and free again. I feel so powerless in this situation. I am weak, but You are strong. Be my strength today. I ask this in the strong name of Your Son, Jesus.

150
Nighttime Anxiety

It's hard for me to go on now, Creator God. I lie awake at night, burdened with anxiety. When I slip into unconsciousness at last, nightmares trouble my sleep. Restore my peace, I pray. Teach me to rest once more in the shadow of Your wings. I know that You let nothing touch me that has not first passed through Your loving hands.

151
Rebuilding My Marriage

❧

I failed my spouse, God. How can I forgive myself? How can I ever hope to be trustworthy again? How can I begin to rebuild what my own hands have broken? I pray that You would give me wisdom, Lord. Show me Your way. Heal me, heal my spouse, heal our marriage. Give us hope for the future.

152
The Problem of Gossip

God, often I don't realize I'm part of the problem when I'm just listening to gossip. I get interested in what's being said and it draws me in slowly. Before I know it, I'm commenting and making assumptions. Sometimes I even pass on the information whether or not I know it's accurate. Please, Father, help me to call this what it is. Gossip. It has no place in my life. Please help me to realize that I'm getting involved sooner and give me the strength to stay out of it.

153
Stress Less; Pray More

❧

I need Your help with this, Father God. I need You to help me find new ways of coping, ways that bring me closer to You. When I'm overwhelmed by life, teach me instead to exercise, to sing, to call someone on the phone, to do something creative, to take a nap. Whatever else You lead me to, be at its center. Use my feelings of stress as the trigger that tells me: Time to pray.

154
Lead Me on Straight Paths

∞

Teach me, Loving Creator, to trust You with all my heart. Help me not to depend on my own understanding. I know that when I seek Your guidance instead, You will lead me on straight paths. I don't want to rely on my own wisdom. Instead, I choose to respect Your Word; I will stay away from anything that pulls me from You. When I do all this, my heart will be at peace—and anxiety will no longer steal my body's health (Proverbs 3).

155
Simply Love

Lord, I know You really don't care how eloquently I present my case; if I don't speak in love, I am like a noisy gong or a clanging cymbal. The love You call me to is patient and kind; it's not arrogant or rude, it doesn't envy or boast, it doesn't insist on its own way, and it's not irritable or resentful (1 Corinthians 13:1–6). Teach me to stop arguing—and instead simply love.

156
This Challenge Is Too Big

❧

The challenge that lies ahead, Lord, is too big for me. My self-confidence fails. I can't help but compare how big the challenge is to my meager abilities for confronting it. My faith wavers. But I know that when I admit how weak I truly am, then You have the chance to reveal Your strength. The challenge that lies ahead shrinks when I compare it to the immensity of You. And I finally realize that my perception of the challenges that lie ahead all depends on my perspective. Keep me focused on You and Your power.

157
Dysfunction in a Relationship

❧

God, I heard it said once that you won't get a different result if you keep doing the same things over and over again. I feel like I'm caught in a bad dream. My loved one and I keep having the same issues, the same fights, the same dysfunction between us. Please give me discernment so that I might see a new way. I'm tired of these same old results.

158
Help from Others

~

God, they made meals, but I could not eat. They sat with me, but I had no words to speak. I don't know how the hours passed because I'm just so numb. But I thank You that they came, these loving servants who have fed my family and run errands and made necessary arrangements. Thank You that they came. They were Your hands and feet today.

159
When Dreams Are Lost

❧

Lord, You know that things haven't turned out as I wanted. You saw the dream as it grew within my heart. You watched me get my hopes up. You were there as I held my breath, hoping for the answer I wanted so desperately. I wonder why You let it all slip through my fingers. Remind me that Your ways are higher than my own (Isaiah 55:8–9) and that You always have my best interest in mind.

160
A Servant's Heart

Jesus, You were a servant leader who even washed Your disciples' feet. Please give me a servant's heart, too. If I need to help my parents with things like bathing or going to the restroom, allow me to know how to assist while helping them feel okay about it. I want them to have their dignity. I love them so.

161

Enduring a Lonely Season

❧

This is a lonely season for me, Father. I remember a time when my life was full of people. Things have changed. I find myself alone more often. Use this season, Lord, to draw me closer to You. Let me fellowship with my Father when I'm alone. As a Christian, I'm never really alone, for You are always near. You will be with me always, even to the end of the age (Matthew 28:20).

162
Time to Move On

My heart is torn, God. Part of me wants to stay, but the other part knows it's time to move on from this place. It's hard to step into the unknown, but I know that You go with me. Please prepare the way for me. I will walk in it. I choose to trust You in this move, Father.

163
Guide My Child Back, Lord

Heavenly Father, my children know Your voice. I taught them about You and took them to church. They know the Bible and its truths. Your sheep know the sound of Your voice. Guide these little ones back to Your ways, Good Shepherd. I ask that You call out to them. I pray that they will heed Your call.

164
I Don't Know What to Do

God, give me wisdom. I don't always know what's best, and everyone has a different opinion on such things as counseling and medication. I know that I need help and admitting it is the first step. Help me to have the presence of mind, even in my depression, to make the best decisions that will help me to get well.

165
Forgiving Myself

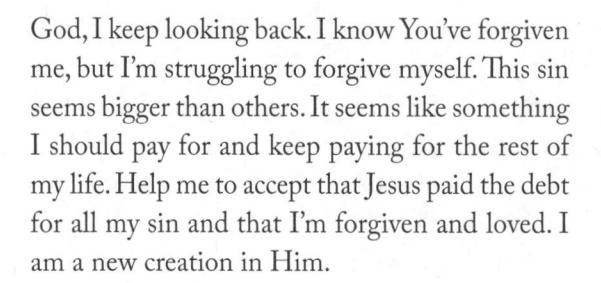

God, I keep looking back. I know You've forgiven me, but I'm struggling to forgive myself. This sin seems bigger than others. It seems like something I should pay for and keep paying for the rest of my life. Help me to accept that Jesus paid the debt for all my sin and that I'm forgiven and loved. I am a new creation in Him.

166
Setting Boundaries

Setting boundaries is so hard for me, Lord. I feel guilty whenever I try to draw a line around myself, whenever I say this far and no farther. Give me wisdom to know which lines need to be drawn, I pray. Give me courage to set boundaries—and then stick with them.

167
Focused on Myself

❧

Loving God, I've noticed that I'm more likely to get angry when I'm focused on myself. I want to be in control—and when I'm not, even little things upset me. Remind me that You are in control, not me. My life is in Your hands. I don't need to feel frustrated when things don't go the way I want. Instead, I can wait to see what new thing You will do.

168
Listening for His Voice

❦

Lord, I know Your voice. Help me to tune into
the voice of my Master, my Good Shepherd (John
10:27), not the other voices that call to me. The
world is full of pleasures that wind up as disasters.
There's a new promise for a greater high or escape
every day in the places I've been living. Help me
to escape this dangerous obstacle course and ex-
change it for the straight paths You've prepared
for me.

169
Scripture's Promises

Father, thank You for Your promises in scripture that I can claim throughout my trials. You promise to never leave me or forsake me. You assure me that nothing—absolutely nothing—has the ability to separate me from Your love (Romans 8:38–39).

170
Lessons Learned from My Pet

God, thank You for giving me my pet and allowing me to learn from this special little one. It seems silly to say that I learned from a pet, but I did. Thank You for the lessons I learned through being loved so completely by an animal. Thank You for the memories. I would do it all over again even though I have to experience this sadness and grief.

171
Waves of Grief

❧

Father, thank You that the waves of grief are just that—waves. Thank You for mercifully seeing to it that there are moments of relief. They're few and far between right now, but they do come. There are moments when I do not cry. There are moments when I'm able to smile or think about something else, if even just long enough to accomplish an everyday task. I thank You for those moments of relief.

172
Remove This Thorn

Just as the apostle Paul prayed for You to remove the thorn from his flesh, I pray for this thorn to be taken from my life. I wait in expectation of what You will do. You will either remove it or You will continue to walk with me through this adversity, using it to strengthen my faith. I trust You, Lord, to do what is best for me.

173

When Jealousy Rears

❧

I know that You don't want me to covet what others have (Exodus 20:17). Jealousy stirs up anger and arguing among even Christian brothers and sisters. Help me to celebrate with others when good things come to them rather than grow jealous or bitter toward them. I want my heart to be right before You and before men.

174
A Spiritual Battle

❦

God, this anxiety is wearing me down. It's a spiritual battle, but it's even taking a physical toll on me. I can't sleep or eat properly. I'm exhausted. Heal my mind and heart. Take away the fear and the panic. Replace them with peace and calm. I long to rest in You. I know that I can't do it on my own. I need You to help me get there, God.

175
Praying for Discernment

Father, I spend so much time trying to decide which is the good, which is the better, and which is the best. I'm juggling too many things. I need Your discernment, Your wisdom, and Your perspective to determine what is best—that is, whatever You want me to do next. Teach me how to say no. Help me figure out what to let go of and what to hold on to. You know what's best for me and the people in my life.

176
A Train Wreck of Worries

❧

God, my thoughts are a train wreck—car after car full of care after care, all banging into each other. I know a lot of it is relatively trivial, but the little things I worry about become bigger issues surrounding the decisions I've made or the people those decisions have affected. I'm calling time out and coming to You with all of it. You care about all the details of my life, and I'm counting on Your peace—which is far beyond my understanding—to keep my mind and thoughts on You and not on my worries (Philippians 4:6–7).

177

Shaken to the Core

❧

God, I need You. I can't make it through the day without You. Things that used to seem easy and mundane are taking all of my brain power in order to accomplish. Everything in my world has been shaken, and it seems so odd that the sun still comes up and everyone is moving on as if nothing happened. Help me make it through each day, Father. I feel so useless and out of control.

178
I Am Not a Failure

The world may call me a failure, but You see it quite differently, Lord. I'm in this world, but I'm not of it. I'm an alien here, for my real home is heaven. When I don't have the largest bank account because I've given freely to others, remind me that money is not the most important thing. When I choose to stay in a place where I'm making an impact for the kingdom, remind me that this honors You. It's okay to let an opportunity for promotion or change pass by if I'm where I feel I should be. In Jesus' name I pray for confidence to do what's right regardless of how the world may view it.

179
Fearing Silly Things

❦

Jesus, I've been afraid. I'm tired of fearing silly things—things that are out of my control. You graciously offer me peace—Your peace. It's a peace the world knows nothing of and cannot offer me. If I simply receive Your peace, I know that my heart will not be troubled or afraid (John 14:27).

180
Yet I Trust You

God, my world seems upside down.

And yet I trust You.

The timing couldn't be worse.

And yet I trust You.

I am overwhelmed with emotion and weariness as I try to deal with these events.

And yet I trust You.

181
I Want to Change

❧

Lord, You know I want to change. And yet again and again, I fall back into the same addictive behaviors. I get so discouraged with myself. Thank You, Lord, that You are never discouraged with me. You are always waiting to give me one more chance.

182
Redeem My Life

❧

I am sick, Lord—and yet I choose to bless Your name. I feel diminished by this illness—and yet I give You all that I have left to offer. Heal me, Lord, if it be Your will. Redeem my life from destruction. Crown me with Your loving-kindness and tender mercies (Psalm 103:1–4).

183
Lying to Myself

❧

Father, sometimes I not only lie to others with my words; I also lie to myself in my thoughts. I criticize myself unjustly. Or I go to the other extreme and excuse myself too easily. I hide unpleasant truths away where I don't have to look at them. Reveal the truth within me, God. Give me the courage to be honest even with myself.

184
The Difficulty of Trust

❧

When I read the Bible, I see, dear God, that I'm not the only one who had a problem trusting. Trust was just as hard for many of the great Bible heroes. Jonah, for example, ended up inside a big fish because he couldn't trust Your commands. Father, thank You that You never abandon me, even when I fail to trust You. Even when I find myself inside life's "big fish," You are there with me. And just as You did with Jonah, You give me another chance.

185
Feeling My Feelings

❧

Dear Jesus, I feel so many things all at the same time. I'm furious and sad, exhausted and frustrated, confused and relieved. Some days I don't feel anything at all, only numbness. Other days I'm filled with anxiety about the future. And then there are the days when I can't stop crying. Thank You that whatever I'm feeling, You're always there with me. You understand me even when I don't understand myself.

186
Anger That Comes Back

❧

Jesus, I try to get rid of my anger, but it keeps coming back. My rage is like a dark stain on a white wall. No matter how many times I try to paint over it, I can still see its mark. And then the paint peels off, and there it is, as dark as ever. Show me how to strip off the stain before I try to paint the wall. Show me the source of my anger. Is it because I am hurt? Or afraid? Is some reaction from my childhood being triggered? Am I jealous and insecure? Am I unsure of my own worth in this situation? Reveal the truth to me, whatever it is—and then heal me, I pray. Only then I will I be able to truly turn from anger.

187

God Is Delivering Me

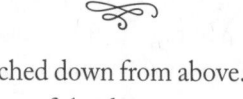

Lord, You reached down from above. You took and drew me up out of the deep waters of depression. You delivered me from my strong enemy, from this depression that was too strong for me to overcome on my own. When calamity seemed to surround me, You held me steady. You brought me forth into a large place, a place of freedom and emotional health. You delivered me, because I delighted You (2 Samuel 22:17–20).

188
God's Power Works in Surprising Ways

~∞~

You told the apostle Paul, Lord, that Your grace was all he needed. Your power, You said, is made perfect in weakness (2 Corinthians 12:9). Remind me to never look down on any form of disability as being weakness. Instead, let me always be open to Your power working in surprising ways.

189
Lessons in Disappointment

❧

Lord, You know how disappointed I feel right now. Remind me, Lord, that I am Your child, and You have a lesson You want me to learn from all this. Help me not to lose heart. I know that even this disappointment comes to me through Your loving hand, because I am Your child. Just as my human parents had to say no to me sometimes, so that I could learn, You, too, are doing what is best for me. You are doing this so that I can grow more like You, so that I can share in Your wholeness. This isn't fun, Lord; in fact, it hurts! But I believe that down the road a ways, I will reap a harvest of peace and righteousness from this disappointment I'm experiencing now (Hebrews 12:5–11).

190
My Family Needs Peace

❧

You offer a peace that the world simply cannot. It's a peace that comes only through a personal walk with Your Son, God. It's a peace that my family needs desperately. Please bless us with a peace that passes all understanding. I ask this in the powerful name of Jesus.

191
More Month than Money

Jesus, money is tight. I seem to run out of it before I run out of days in the month. Please take what I have and stretch it. Give me wisdom in my spending and in places I can cut back. Ultimately, help me to trust You with this money. It's all Yours anyway.

192
I Choose to. . .

Some trust in chariots or horses. I trust in the name of the Lord my God (Psalm 20:7). I choose to walk in the strength of my Savior. I choose to rest in my Redeemer. I choose to endure because of Emmanuel—God with us. God before me. God with me. God beside me.

193
Past, Present, and Future

God, I give You my present and my future because I know You can handle them better than I ever could. You have shown up in my past and provided for my every need. You have filled my life with blessings. Help me to trust You with the unknown by banking on what I do know—You are a faithful God.

194
Soul Healing

❧

I know, Lord, that You don't always choose to heal those who are ill. Sometimes instead, You ask sick people to bear their infirmary. And yet even then, I believe You bring healing, the deepest healing that reaches to the depths of a person's soul and lasts until eternity. God, I ask You for that kind of healing. You know I wish I could be free of this illness, here, now (right now!), in this life. But give me the strength to bear it, if instead, You will heal me in other ways, ways I need even more.

195
I Surrender My Body to You, Lord

~~~

God, don't let sin reign in my flesh, in the form of drugs or anything else. I don't want to obey anything that has to do with sin. I don't want my body to be used for anything but Your righteousness. I give myself to You; in fact, I give You my entire body to use as Your instrument. I don't want sin to have any dominion over me, for I know that Your grace is mine (Romans 6:12–14).

196
Something Good Ahead

❧

Lord, remind me of what is most important. It would be easy to pray that You would restore my finances, but instead I pray for courage, self-confidence, and humility: the courage, self-confidence, and humility to start over again; enough courage, self-confidence, and humility to face the embarrassment I feel when others know the situation I'm in; and the courage, self-confidence, and humility to believe that You still have something good for me ahead. Remind me that Your love for me never wavers, no matter what my finances are.

197
God's Spirit in My Words

❦

May I use my conversations only for Your glory,
Lord. Remind me to seek to bless others with
each thing I say. If arguments and cross words
pour out of me, how can I claim to be filled with
Your Spirit? Your Word tells us that a salt pond
cannot yield fresh water, nor can a fig tree bear
olives (James 3:12). Cleanse my heart first, dear
God, and then my mouth and all its words, so that
my life is not filled with contradiction.

198

My Father Fights for Me

❦

You have given me a spirit of power, of love, and of self-discipline (2 Timothy 1:7). I am not alone. You go with me into battle. The battle is not my own. It belongs to my God. I refuse to fear. I call on the powerful name of God Almighty to see me through. Thank You for fighting for me, Lord.